The Pathway to Finding Purpose and True Happiness

Sherdeine Thomas

The Pathway to Finding Purpose and True Happiness.
Copyright © 2018. Sherdeine Thomas. All Rights Reserved.

Printed in the United States of America.

No portion of this book may be reproduced, stored in a retrieval system, or transmitted in any form or by any means, except for brief quotations in printed reviews, without the prior written permission of Sherdeine Thomas and DayeLight Publishers.

Unless otherwise indicated, all scripture quotations are taken from the King James Version.

Book Cover Design by HCP Book Publishing

ISBN: 978-0-9997404-2-2

Dedication

This book is dedicated to those who are on the journey of fulfilling a purpose-driven life. You know you were called to live a life of greatness and to make an impact on the next generation.

If you have ever felt broken, confused, and stuck on a path, unsure of your calling on earth, then *The Pathway to Finding Purpose and True Happiness* is dedicated to you.

If you have started your journey but need someone to guide you along the path that leads to your divine purpose and destiny, then *The Pathway to Finding Purpose and True Happiness* is dedicated to you.

This book is dedicated to all who are on a journey to finding true joy and happiness by living a purpose-driven life.

You were created to accomplish a purpose; you were created with a master blueprint; you were created as a purpose-driven being; you were created to fulfill the master plan God has for your life. Your life is valuable, and you exist today for a reason; that reason is called purpose.

Acknowledgements

I want to first and foremost acknowledge my Heavenly Father, who is the head of my life and the Author and Finisher of my faith. Thank you, Lord, for giving me the wonderful privilege of using the gift of writing to minister to the hearts of your people.

To my mom, Beverley Casillo, thank you for being a source of strength.

To my friends, who encouraged me through this season, thank you for believing in me.

To my supporters, well-wishers, brothers, and sisters in the faith, thank you for all your tremendous support and continuous prayers.

To Crystal Daye, COO of DayeLight International Publishing Company and team, thank you for bringing this book to life.

Acknowledgments

Table of Contents

Dedication iii
Acknowledgements v
Introduction 1
    The Search 2
    The Birth of Purpose 2

Chapter 1
Understanding the Truth Behind Your Life 5
    There is Glory in Your Suffering 6
    Allows His Peace to Speak to Your Mind 6
    This Can Only be Found in His Word 7

Chapter 2
The Journey to Living a Better Life 9
    The Courage Walk 11
    The Hidden Pain 12
    Don't Give Up 12
    He is the Way 13

Chapter 3
He Knows Your Needs 15
    Why Worry? 16
    Will you Surrender? 17
    Receive the FREE GIFT of Eternal Life 18
    Accept the Challenge 18
    Take the Faith Walk 19
    The Gratitude of Giving Thanks 19

Chapter 4
The Power of Prayer 21
    Developing Intimacy With God...21
    Understanding the Power You Have in Purpose 22
    A Prayer for Breaking the Chain of Bondages....................23
    We Need Him to Carry Out His Ultimate Plans 24
    Making God the Center of Your Life Will
    Change Your Path 24
    Place Your Life in His Hands..24

Chapter 5
The Test... 27
    Testimony 28

Chapter 6
Get Connected to the Source 31
    Who is the Holy Spirit?..31
    When You Pray, Listen, Because God Speaks....................35
    Develop a Mindset That You Will Live
    a Life of Purpose..36
    Prevail and Break Through Into Your Purpose.................37

Chapter 7
Your Attitude Will Determine Your Altitude..................... 39
    Enduring Suffering 41
    Change Your Jar..42
    Develop the Right Attitude 43

Chapter 8
Walking In Your Purpose 45
    Get Connected to the Source 46
    What is Your Purpose?...46
    Your Soul Connects Your Purpose 48
    How Can I Fulfill My Purpose?...49

Chapter 9
Be Still and Know That He Is God 55
    Do Not Complain 56
    Mirror Challenge 59
    Your Life is Worth Living 59
    He Had Me In His Plans 60
    You Are In His Plans 60
    His Plans 60
    Key Notes 61

Chapter 10
Reposition Your Life to the Will of God 65
    Take A Stand 67
    The Change Must Begin With You 67
    Shift Your Mindset 68

Chapter 11
The Beauty of Trusting God 71
    You Must Decrease So God Can Increase 72
    You Must Give Up To Gain 73
    Trusting In God Brings Inner Peace 73
    Purpose Cannot Fail 75

Chapter 12
Living A Life of Blessings and Miracles 77
    Man's Rejection is God's Appointment 77
    You Will Be Rejected In Order To Be Appointed 78
    Rejection Leads To A Life Of Miracles And Blessings 79

Chapter 13
What Awaits a Life of Purpose and True Happiness? 81
    His Power Works Through Us 81
    Experience The Walk 82

Make a note of it: 82
Testimony 83
God's Promises Bring Forth Protection 84
His Manifestation Produces Power 86

Chapter 14
Remain In The Waiting Period of God's Timing 91
The Season 92
All For God's Glory 92
The Season Is Never Lost Forever 93
Remain In The Season 93
Avoid Making The Wrong Move 93
Allow God To Heal You During Your Season 94
The Outcome Is Always Greater 96
To Every Season, There Is A Reason 96

Chapter 15
Living On Purpose By Answering The Call 99
My Testimony 100
God Does Not Need Our Assistance 101
He Comforted My Soul 101
Conclusion 105
About the Author 107

Introduction

The Pathway to Finding Purpose and True Happiness was written to equip, empower, motivate, inspire, and transform the lives of those who are on a quest to discover their purpose and desire to live a life of true happiness.

Life before purpose for the author was meaningless, and even though she was active in church, part of her wanted more. Hence, this yearning took her on a journey to finding purpose and true happiness.

Can you imagine living in a world that dictates to you, tells you how to act, dress, live, and look. The author took on the pattern of the world. She tried to be perfect in the eyes of man. She tried everything to live a life that was not created for her. This gave her an inner sadness; it created an empty void no one could fill.

One day, she decided to become the person God created her to be, but she had no idea how to become that person. She purposed in her heart to seek the One who created her.

You may be on your journey to finding purpose and true happiness. You may have started your journey but still need someone to hold your hand and guide you along the path.

This book was written with you in mind. Every chapter and word in this book was written for you.

The Pathway to Finding Purpose and True Happiness will not just guide you, but it will connect with you spiritually, physically, and emotionally- on a personal level.

If you were given one chance to transform one of your heart's desires, would you allow that chance to pass you by? This is your chance; it's called purpose. Let the author take your hand and walk you along this path by **FAITH**. Approach each chapter with an open mind and a willingness to discover the plans and the purpose God has for your life.

Your destiny awaits **YOU**.
Your future depends on **YOU**.
Purpose is ready to take **YOU** on a new journey.

The Search

There are times we search for true happiness in the heart of a loved one, friend, children, spouse, family, or money. But we will never find true happiness until we begin to walk in our purpose.

The Birth of Purpose

Everything that you hope, dream of, or imagine is attached to your purpose. Purpose brings true happiness. Purpose is the steering wheel to living a God-ordained life that will cause you to find the happiness you have been searching for all your life.

Imagine your life now, then imagine what you desire your life to look like. Write these thoughts down. Now write beside it **Purpose.**

If you follow your PURPOSE, you will walk into your destiny. Wouldn't you be excited to know what your destiny is? We all have a guide in front of us. The problem is, we tend to look too far trying to find it when it is right in front of us.

The Pathway to Finding Purpose and True Happiness will guide you into your destiny, so you can live the life created for you.

Today, I want you to imagine purpose as your hand tool; imagine purpose as your guide and picture it as the ultimate driver behind your wheel. Purpose will guide you toward your destination. Those who live a purpose-driven life are not easily distracted because their purpose connects them to the source of life (Jesus).

Jesus saith unto him, I am the way, the truth, and the life: no man cometh unto the Father, but by me **(John 14:6 – KJV).**

Purpose connects you with the source. The source connects you to the plans and the purpose God has for you, and His plans now become your ultimate goal in life.

Make a list of your goals and write your purpose (as far as you know).

_____

_____

_____

_____

_____

_____

_____

It took me thirty years to understand that true happiness is not found in the world or in the situations we face daily. It is found when we dedicate our lives to living for the One who gave up His life to save us from our sins. **John 3:16 says**: "For God so loved the world, that he gave his only begotten Son, that whosoever believeth in him should not perish, but have everlasting life."

> Our current situation does not stop God's plans from coming to pass. Paul states it perfectly, "Who hath saved us, and called us with an holy calling, not according to our works, but according to his own purpose and grace, which was given us in Christ Jesus before the world began" **(2 Timothy 1:9)**.

As you read this life-transforming book, dedicate yourself to fulfilling the ultimate purpose God created you for, so you can begin to live the life that will transform you and lead you to true happiness. May the peace of God reign in you as He leads you to find the ultimate plans and purpose for which you were created.

CHAPTER 1

Understanding the Truth Behind Your Life

Is the life we desire the life God has for us? In today's society, everyone aspires to live a life free from stress and worries and all the daily struggles. Don't we all imagine that life? I do! For years I searched for a life that would take me away from the pain, sorrow, sadness, depression, and failure. God did not promise us a life free from stress, worries, and struggles. He reminds us in His word:

Beloved, think it not strange concerning the fiery trial which is to try you, as though some strange thing happened unto you: But rejoice, inasmuch as ye are partakers of Christ's sufferings; that, when his glory shall be revealed, ye may be glad also with exceeding joy. If ye be reproached for the name of Christ, happy are ye; for the spirit of glory and of God resteth upon you: on their part he is evil spoken of, but on your part he is glorified. **(1 Peter 4:12-14 – KJV)**.

What an assurance we have while suffering. I wish I had understood the depth of this text in my early years of developing intimacy with God. All those years wasted feeling sorry for myself and drowning in self-pity, sadness, and depression.

There is Glory in Your Suffering

The pain you are feeling now, the rejection, the trials, the brokenness, the loneliness, the confusion, God is saying to you right now: Don't be surprised, don't be worried, don't get depressed, don't think it is something strange, don't think I have forgotten about you, don't think I have left you hopeless.

Yes, the pain is real, the scars are real, the tears are real, the feeling is real. You can see it; you can feel it but believe in My promises. Hold on to My words. Trust the process. It is I, God, who allowed this to come upon you, so you will see my hands at work in your life and you will glorify Me as your Creator and Heavenly Father.

Rejoice in your suffering, allow Me to birth purpose through you. I will release an uncommon anointing inside you that will flow rivers of living water; you won't have room to contain my blessing.

Allows His Peace to Speak to Your Mind

In pursuit of finding purpose and true happiness, confusion will arise, but abide steadfastly in His promise. He promises to give unto you the peace that surpasses all human understanding (See **Philippians 4:7**).

What an amazing joy to know that amid your adversity and trials, God will allow you to stay focused and His joy will flood your soul.

Do you desire to have peace in your life? Do you desire to experience the love of God? Do you desire to reach a place in your life where you know that no matter what circumstances and situations arise, deep inside your heart you know God is there steering you toward a life of purpose and true happiness?

Yes, we all need that assurance at some point in our walk as we discover what we are truly placed on earth to accomplish.

This Can Only be Found in His Word

Your purpose and true happiness can only be found in salvation. **Jeremiah 29:13 says**: "And ye shall seek me, and find me, when ye shall search for me with all your heart."

Are you seeking God with all your heart? Let the search begin in the mind. The steps to seeking God begins with a transformation of the mind and a releasing of the Word of God through your soul. Begin to transform and activate the power of God in your mind by releasing the Word of God in your spirit. I guarantee you will know the heart of God and your purpose will be birthed.

Now let us go on a journey together to finding purpose and true happiness. It's already done, and we will find it together.

Make a list of the deep things God is revealing to you right now:

_____

_____

_____

_____

_____

_____

Let's Pray:

Father in the name of Jesus, I pray that You will prepare my heart, mind, body, and soul to experience You in a new way, even now. Holy Spirit, rest on me. Open my mind to receive the blessing You have in store for me. In Jesus' name. Amen.

CHAPTER 2

The Journey to Living a Better Life

Living a better life is a choice and a journey that one must embark on for oneself. The journey to finding purpose and true happiness does not happen overnight, as many of us hope or desire; instead, it is a process, an extended period of molding and making and pruning. This may take months or even years, but during this time, we must seek to develop the ability to trust the One who created us. It begins by analyzing where you are as an individual, doing the introspection needed to evaluate your life, recognizing that you are not satisfied with the person you are and taking steps to make a change.

Have you ever evaluated your life and said: There must be a better way of life, there must be something different from this pain I am experiencing, there must be a ray of hope, there must be laughter in the sunshine and fulfillment in life.

You may have thought: God must have something greater than this for me; and I need to find it. If you have ever had any of these thoughts, then you are searching for purpose and true happiness. Now let me introduce you to the only One who can lead you into living the life you were created to live.

We are reminded in **John 14:6**: 'Jesus saith unto him, I am the way, the truth, and the life: no man cometh unto the Father, but by me.'" There is no other way to finding true happiness than to enter through the door of Jesus Christ, which leads to eternal life through Salvation.

> *Let's Pray:*
>
> *Father, I have acknowledged that there is no other way to come to You but through Your Son Jesus Christ; therefore Lord, I ask that You to grant me eternal salvation through Your son Jesus Christ. Help me to understand that You are the truth and the light. Forgive me of all my sins and take me into full communion with You through the blessed Holy Spirit. Pour Your anointing over my life and guide me into finding true salvation through You. In Jesus' name I pray. Amen.*

If you have prayed this prayer and you are not saved, I implore you to visit a nearby church built upon the foundation of Jesus Christ. Let them guide you to the next process of giving your life to God.

If you are saved and not sure about your identity in Christ, then open your heart and allow Jesus to enter and renew you with the love of the Holy Spirit.

If you have identified your purpose and need guidance, allow God to lead you to live a purpose-driven life.

2 Peter 3:9 reminds us: "The Lord is not slack concerning his promise, as some men count slackness; but is longsuffering to us-ward, not willing that any should perish, but that all should come to repentance."

The Lord loves you and He cares deeply for you. What amazes me about Jesus is that He is such a forgiving God. His arms are wide open just waiting to hug you and show you how much He loves you with an everlasting love. God loves you so much. Yes, you. You reading this right now—He cares for YOU. His desire is that you will begin to live a purpose-driven life, so you can find true happiness by the power of His Holy Spirit.

Now pause for a moment and tell Him how much you love Him.

The Courage Walk

It takes courage to reach the point where you say to yourself: I am not satisfied with who I am, I am not satisfied with where I am. I know there is better in store for me and I am now willing to take the necessary steps to take me to where God desires me to be.

When you reach this point, then you know you are ready to be transformed for God's purpose and plans for your life.

The reality is, we often go through a stressful period in life where we feel as if we cannot make it. There are moments when we choose to give up because we are unable to contain the pain and hurt that has built up on the inside.

Have you ever been at a point where you were so tired from all the cares of life that you needed someone to lean on, someone to give you one word of encouragement? Sometimes all you desire is a shoulder to cry on. I understand because I have been there too. I have endured moments when I just wish I could lay in someone's arms and pour out and release all the clogged-up tears and pain.

The Hidden Pain

Sometimes you try to explain what is going through your mind, but no one understands because they expect you to have it all together. But Jesus doesn't expect you to have it all together. **No**, he knows there will be times when you feel so all alone, and you need someone to lean on. At this time, His desire is that you will lean on Him, you will take the courage walk and allow Him to show you the path that He has created for you long before you existed.

There is a way out; there is a path that was established long before you and I were created. All it takes is a walk of courage to say, "Lord, I will trust You to lead me to this path." Allow God to take you on this journey because just when we feel like all hope is gone, there is a little courage on the inside that tells us to hold on a little longer, dig a little deeper and take Jesus at His Word. If you are at this stage, then allow courage to push you out by faith.

Don't Give Up

There are moments when you will be tempted to give up. **Don't give up**—you must push your way through. Pushing begins in the mind. When a mother is about to give birth, her mind tells the body, "**Hey,** listen, the baby is here, so get ready to push." The mind knows when you are under attack, so we must first develop the strength and courage in the mind. When you have developed this strength and courage, you now give way to God to fill the empty gap- the God-sized void that only He can fill.

He is the Way

Trying to fill an empty gap is like pouring water into a broken cup. The more you pour the water into the broken cup, the more the water leaks out, because the gap in the cup needs mending. We often experience stress and brokenness in our life, but until we allow God to mend the open gap in the cup, we will never be able to contain the water.

You may ask: How can I fill this broken gap? **Matthew 6:25** tells us we should not worry about what we shall eat or drink because our Heavenly Father knows what we need before we even ask. Maybe your needs are not food, clothing, shelter, or drink. the beauty is, whatever your needs are, He promises to supply. **Philippians 4:19**: "But my God shall supply all your need according to his riches in glory by Christ Jesus."

Do you have a need to be filled? Make a note of that need and join me in prayer.

_____

_____

_____

_____

_____

_____

_____

_____

> *Let's Pray:*
>
> *Father, here is Your child's need. You promised that if two or three persons come together and agree on anything in Your name, You are in the midst. Now, Lord, we may not be in the same space, but by faith we come in agreement on the prayers raised and stand firmly on Your words. Trusting that in your wisdom you will answer as only You can. We know that all things are possible to those who believe. Heavenly Father, we believe it is already done. We believe this need is met according to the plans and purpose You have for Your child's life.*

If you have prayed this prayer, then believe God by faith and receive your breakthrough in Jesus' name.

CHAPTER 3

He Knows Your Needs

If our heavenly Father knows our needs, then what is the next step for us to take? Should we live a life of defeat? No!

Depression has become the number one issue in today's society and the enemy uses it to blind the minds of the children of God and to shift their focus off the ultimate prize, which is living for God.

I believe we can overcome any mental, physical, or psychological problem that hampers our lives. **Philippians 4:13** gives us the assurance that we can do all things through Christ who strengths us.

Roman 8:37 tells us that in all things we are more than conquerors through Him that loves us. If we believe in the Word of God, then we are on our way to defeating the plans of the enemy and positioning ourselves to live a purpose-driven life.

Some days struggles may weigh us down. But Jesus asks a profound question in **Matthew 6:27,** "Which of you by taking thought can add one cubit unto his stature?"

The answer is no; we cannot add a minute to our life. We cannot solve our problems by worrying, neither can we stop the pain. Worrying about the obstacles in life will not solve or mend any of life's concerns.

Why Worry?

Take a few minutes and ask yourself, "Can worry change my current situation?" Write down your answer. I am assuming that the answer is No.

If you have reached this point in the book, then the next step for you is to say, "Today is the last day I will worry about any issue I may be facing. I choose to place it in the hands of God and allow Him to guide my mind into His grace."

Consider this popular hymn before we pray:

> All to Jesus I surrender,
> All to Him I freely give;
> I will ever love and trust Him,
> In His presence daily live.
> I surrender all,
> I surrender all.
> All to Thee, my blessed Savior,
> I surrender all.
> All to Jesus I surrender,
> Humbly at His feet I bow,
> Worldly pleasures all forsaken;
> Take me, Jesus, take me now.
> All to Jesus I surrender,
> Make me, Savior, wholly Thine;
> Let me feel Thy Holy Spirit,
> Truly know that Thou art mine.
> All to Jesus I surrender,

> Lord, I give myself to Thee;
> Fill me with Thy love and power,
> Let Thy blessing fall on me.
> All to Jesus I surrender,
> Now I feel the sacred flame.
> Oh, the joy of full salvation!
> Glory, glory to His name!

Will You Surrender?

Surrendering all to Jesus is a self-sacrifice that only you can make for yourself. It takes giving up your own will and allowing God's will to be done in your life. It takes total submission and slaying of self-will to surrender. The best part about doing this is, if you are willing to give it all up for Jesus, you don't have to do it alone. You have the Father, the Son, and the Holy Spirit—the blessed comforter who will gently take your hands and lead you into a purpose-driven life that guarantees great joy and true happiness.

Let's Pray:

Father, we humbly come to You, putting our own will at the altar of sacrifice. We ask that You align our will with Your will through the power of the Holy Spirit. We know it is not by might nor by power, but it is by Your Spirit. Bless us even now, Lord, and take away our sinful desire and replace it with Your tender mercy and love. Breathe afresh upon us even now as we tell You thanks in Jesus' name. Amen.

Receive the FREE GIFT of Eternal Life

Accept this free gift. Close your eyes for a few seconds and by faith accept Jesus Christ as your Lord, Savior, and soon coming king.

> It is a simple command, but it carries a heavy weight. "But without faith it is impossible to please him: for he that cometh to God must believe that he is, and that he is a rewarder of them that diligently seek him." (**Hebrews 11:6**).

Take a few seconds and tell God that you surrender all to Him and lay all your worries in His hands. Whisper a prayer of confession in your heart and ask Him to forgive you of all your sins.

Begin to trust the Holy Spirit as He guides and lead you into fulfilling your divine purpose.

Accept the Challenge

Make a promise to yourself that each day you will stay positive, think positive, and try to surround yourself with positive energy.

Begin each day by feasting on the Word of God. Pray for new insights and for His leading in your life. Ask God to take full control of your day. Ask Him to take control of every thought that enters your mind. Try to recite at least one encouraging Bible verse per day—this will help you stay positive and it will also give the Holy Spirit easier access to lead you on your journey to finding purpose.

> **James 1:2-4**: My brethren, count it all joy when ye fall into divers temptations; knowing this, that the trying of your faith worketh patience. But let patience have her perfect work, that ye may be perfect and entire, wanting nothing.

> **Romans 1:17:** For therein is the righteousness of God revealed from faith to faith: as it is written, The just shall live by faith.

Take the Faith Walk

Take your faith and your spiritual life to the next level by trusting God completely and depending on Him to carry you through. Always remember that God will make a way for you even when there seems to be no way. Access the possible faith, for there is nothing impossible with God.

The Gratitude of Giving Thanks

Finally, develop a heart of thanksgiving. Thank God for even the simplest daily blessing.

> **Psalm 100:4-5:** Enter into his gates with thanksgiving, and into his courts with praise: be thankful unto him, and bless his name. For the Lord is good; his mercy is everlasting; and his truth endureth to all generations.

CHAPTER 4

The Power of Prayer

Prayer is one of the most essential tools when trying to find your purpose. Through constant prayer, you will be able to communicate with God. When we communicate with God, we allow His Spirit to guide our hearts in making the correct decisions.

The beauty of communicating with the Creator far surpasses human understanding. It is said that prayer is a two-way process. We talk, God listens, then He speaks to us. Imagine the Creator of heaven and earth giving you His full attention. No wonder the enemy tries so hard to block our prayer life because he knows the power that God's children have when we begin to pray. Through prayer we acquire power; and its through power purpose is birth.

Developing Intimacy With God

When I understood how effective prayer was, my prayer life began to transform. Yes, and yours will transform too. Prayer is your weapon, and you can use the weapon to conquer the plans of the enemy over your life.

> **Genesis 1:26 says:** And God said, Let us make man in our image, after our likeness: and let them have dominion over the fish of the sea, and over the fowl of the air, and over the cattle, and over all the earth, and over every creeping thing that creepeth upon the earth.

Now the keyword in this scripture is **DOMINION**.

Understanding the Power You Have in Purpose

Dominion means sovereignty or control, authority, rulership. God has given you the authority over anything taking root that is not in alignment with God's plan and purpose for your life. You have authority, through the power of the Holy Spirit, to pull down any stronghold in your life through prayer. You have the authority to command the atmosphere to shift in your favor.

> In **Joshua 10:12,** Joshua commanded the sun to stand still, and it stood still. What is taking root in your life that needs to stand still? Take authority over it so that your purpose can be birthed through the power of the Holy Spirit.

Jesus gave a good example when He cursed the fig tree in **Mark 11:12-25**. It was not the season for the fig tree to bear fruit, but Jesus still cursed it because He was hungry. Jesus displayed an example of faith and what faith can and will do.

It may not be your season, but God is saying to you: "I have given you authority by the Holy Spirit to shift things in your favor." Stop taking your prayer life so lightly and lift your faith by allowing God's purpose to be birthed in you.

Before we pray, picture anything that is taking root in your life that makes you feel uncomfortable and is causing pain and hurt. Picture any situation that needs to change and needs to be shifted out of your life. It could be a new job or house, bills, sickness, or reclaiming your spouse. Whatever it is, imagine it in your mind. Now invite the Spirit of God into your heart and begin to magnify the name of Jesus and give Him praise. Ask Him to forgive you of your sins and cleanse you from all unrighteousness.

A Prayer for Breaking the Chains of Bondage

Let's Pray:

Father, in the name of Jesus, we break every chain that has Your reader captive. We bind every plan of the enemy over Your children's lives. We speak to the atmosphere and we command it to shift in Your children's favor. We call forth healing of the mind, heart, body, and soul. We declare blessing and prosperity over their lives. We command broken families to be mended; we speak life into every dead situation that is not Your will; we call them forth to life right now so that purpose will be birthed in Jesus' name. Amen. **(Repeat this prayer aloud)**

We Need Him to Carry Out His Ultimate Plans

Always remember that God can do without us—He doesn't need us to survive, but we cannot do without Him—we need Him to survive. I love how the Psalmist put it **Psalm 8:4**: "What is man, that thou art mindful of him? and the son of man, that thou visitest him?" We are nothing, yet still He cares for us and gave up His only Son to die to save us from sin. What an awesome God we serve; so kind, loving, and merciful.

Making God the Center of Your Life Will Change Your Path

I have learned to depend on Jesus and take Him at His Word and trust Him in everything I do. I want you to make God your number one priority, your number one goal in life. He should be first in your life; there should not be anything or anyone before God.

Building my life around God has shaped me into the woman I am today: a minister of the Gospel, Author, Transformational Speaker, a Purpose Breakthrough Coach, and Kingdom Entrepreneur of Visionaries International Coaching. Purpose did this and purpose will do it for you.

Place Your Life in His Hands

When you place your life in God's hands, He will transform you into the person He desires you to be—not the person your parents, friends, or family expected you to be, not even the person you think you should be, but the person He created you to be.

Growing up, my dad wanted me to become a nurse. Many people told me I fit the post of a teacher, and I thought I would become the CEO/Marketing Manager of a big company. Being an Author/Minister/ Purpose breakthrough Coach and a Kingdom Entrepreneur was nowhere on my mind. All these came to pass when I began to seek after God's heart.

Will you forget about your plans and allow God's plans and purpose to come to pass in your life? Only His plans for our lives matter because it is the ultimate reason you were created.

Allowing God to transform my life was one of the best things I have ever done. Not only did He make this old clay over, He showed her what her true purpose was. He showed her that she could only find true happiness by totally surrendering to Him.

Do you desire to give Him your life? Then do so by totally surrendering your heart to Him.

Let's Pray:

Heavenly Father, we come to You in total submission to Your will, asking You to bring our lives into alignment with Your will for us in Christ Jesus. Amen.

CHAPTER 5
The Test

One of the most difficult journeys to finding purpose and true happiness is the journey of testing. This is a moment when many people feel as if God has forgotten about them. It is during this difficult time we tend to turn our back on God because the pain, brokenness, heartache, sickness, and confusion is so intense, we allow it to cloud our mind and thoughts. These thoughts shift our focus from God because He is silent during this time.

If you have ever been through this journey, then you can relate to what I am talking about. Even if you are currently going through this journey, then you can also relate. During this period, it is best to lean on the strength of God and trust the process and not the pain. Breakthrough your pain and propel into your purpose.

> **1 Peter 1:7:** That the trial of your faith, being much more precious than of gold that perisheth, though it be tried with fire, might be found unto praise and honour and glory at the appearing of Jesus Christ:

If God is allowing you to go through a test, then rest assured that He has an ultimate plan waiting for you to propel you into your purpose.

Testimony

When God tests you, it is always to make you stronger. God tests you, but the devil tempts you. No wonder the devil is known as the tempter. There is a difference between testing and tempting. I will break down the differences in the next chapter.

God tests each of us in different ways. He knows just how much we can manage and the level at which to give us our testing. In our eyes, testing is painful because it brings much pain and sometimes even suffering. But it helps to build the spiritual man inside of us and it takes us into a new dimension to knowing who God is and what God can do. To fulfill your purpose and to walk into true happiness, you must endure some form of testing. This will be a testimony for you to speak about the goodness of God upon your life. It is through testing, your testimony comes.

When I gave my life to the Lord at age 25, I was so healthy, with absolutely no sickness. Shortly after I gave my life to the Lord, I had a dream of a person who represented the devil. In the vision, he was inflicting illness on people. I remember vividly when he looked at me and said, "You are next." I immediately woke from the dream so frightened, not knowing what to do. Fear took hold of my life.

A few weeks after the dream, I became ill. I remember waking in the middle of the night with sweat running down my body and my heart pounding so fast I felt like I was about to die. This started happening so frequently that I became scared. Upon visiting my physician, he told me it was an anxiety attack.

This took a hold of my life both physically and spiritually. I was drained. It became so bad even to the point where I became afraid of traveling alone. The thought of death took over my life. I decided to seek God for comfort, healing, and deliverance. I had done numerous heart tests and they kept coming back normal. I started praying harder and fasting more because I knew that God could and would heal me.

A few months later, during my prayer and fasting, I realized that this was a test from God. He allowed the enemy to attack me, so I would be drawn closer to Him and to make me stronger in Him. We never know why God allows things, but we must understand that God knows exactly what He is doing.

One thing I also realized during this journey of testing is that God allowed the enemy to use the thing I was most fearful about (sickness and death). The enemy used that fear to try to pull me from God. But it is so amazing that even when the enemy tries to do evil, God turns it around for good. Your testing will allow you to prove who God is. The enemy can only do what God allows him to do. This reminds me of the book of Job.

Job was a man who feared God. He loved God and gave God his all. But the enemy believed Job feared and loved God because of the things God gave him. The book of Job also tells us that Job was rich in everything—cattle, land, money, and children—just to name a few. Job had everything his heart desired.

The enemy wanted God to test Job's love and sincerity for Him. So, the enemy went to God one day and asked permission to touch Job because he wanted to prove a point. But God knew Job loved Him and his heart was sincere for Him, so God gave the enemy permission to touch Job. Even during his affliction, Job still held his ground (**Hold your ground**). The Bible reminds us that even Job's wife told him to curse God and die. Job lost everything; even his friends, who should have comforted him, accused him of doing something wrong.

Despite the enemy causing affliction on Job, he sinned not. We might wonder why God allowed the enemy to touch us or our families or surroundings, but hold your ground like Job because your testing will bring out your purpose and your purpose will allow you to live a life that contains true happiness.

The testing I have been through has shaped my life into being the phenomenal woman I am today. I must emphasize how amazing aligning your life with purpose is. Before purpose, I was empty, lost, and aimless. Today, I am purpose-driven and living the life I was created to live. Purpose allowed me to be able to bless you. Get in line with purpose so **GOD** can use you to bless the heart of all those who are waiting for you.

Allow your testing to mold you into your purpose. Your future depends on it—your happiness awaits you. **Break through your pain and propel into your purpose.**

Let's Pray:

Heavenly Father, may You allow me to stand firmly in my faith and break through my pain so that I will propel into the plans and the purpose You have created me for. In Jesus' name. Amen

CHAPTER 6

Get Connected to the Source

Surrendering leads to great sacrifice. The dictionary defines the word 'surrendering' as the means of giving up something completely. The act of surrendering frees you up to achieve what God wants to achieve through you. The moment you begin to surrender your life to God is the moment when you give God complete access to your life.

God will not bring to pass the plans and the purpose He has for your life until He has complete access. Can I go a little deeper into access? Access is the means or approach to entering a place. The place is your body; the means of approach/access is through the power of the Holy Spirit.

Who is the Holy Spirit?

John 14:26 - But the Comforter, which is the Holy Ghost, whom the Father will send in my name, he shall teach you all things, and bring all things to your remembrance, whatsoever I have said unto you.

Jesus promised to send the believer a Comforter, who is the Holy Spirit, to lead us into all truth. When we surrender, we give the Holy Spirit complete access to our mortal body. The spirit of God now begins to live on the inside of our body. "What? know ye not that your body is the temple of the Holy Ghost which is in you, which ye have of God, and ye are not your own?" (**1 Corinthians 6:19**).

> Our bodies do not belong to us; our bodies are the house/temple of the Holy Spirit. For the Holy Spirit to live inside, you must "present your bodies a living sacrifice, holy, acceptable unto God, *which is* your reasonable service." (**Romans 12:1**).

I love how Paul puts it—a living sacrifice. A sacrifice cannot be dead. There is nowhere in the Old Testament that tells the story of the great men offering dead sacrifices unto God. Abraham was so obedient to God that he was willing to give up his son as a living sacrifice unto God. **Genesis 22** tells the story.

What is so significant about offering a living sacrifice? Sacrifice is defined as the act of giving up something that you want to keep, especially to get or do something else or to help someone.

Let us break down the first part: it is the act of giving up something that you want to keep. The significance of offering a living sacrifice is:

1. **The ability to give up willpower.** The one thing that men fight over is willpower; the one thing that our nations fight over is the ability to have willpower—the ability to rule. When you present a living sacrifice, you give up your willpower.

There is no greater sacrifice we can make as human beings than to give up our willpower. It takes everything inside you to give up the power of rulership. When you have reached the point in your life where you can let go and let God, then you give God complete access to bring His plans and purpose to pass in your life.

A purposeful life is a walk of total surrender to God. In this walk of faith, you now **vow** to present your life as a living sacrifice to Him. You begin to surrender, so the Holy Spirit can have complete access to your body so that His work here on earth can come to pass. Your purpose is not for you; it is your God-given work to do on earth to accomplish the plans of the One who created you.

Jesus' ultimate plan was to set up God's kingdom on earth. In His prayer, He teaches us to say, "Thy kingdom come. Thy will be done in earth, as *it is* in heaven" (Matthew 6:10). What does He want done on earth?

God's desire for us as His children is to operate in the kingdom He has established here on earth. His kingdom is established to carry out His Father's will.

John 6:40: "And this is the will of him that sent me, that every one which seeth the Son, and believeth on him, may have everlasting life: and I will raise him up at the last day."

In this kingdom here on earth, we all have a role to play, and this role is established through **walking in our purpose**. By walking in our purpose, we will begin to do the **will of God**. When we begin to do His will, then our hope of finding true happiness will be accomplished. Everything aligned to your future to proper you into greatness, success, and happiness is connected to your purpose.

Begin to walk in your purpose and you will find true happiness. You were created for one purpose only and that purpose is to carry out the ultimate plans that God has for your life.

Living a life of obedience will lead you to finding purpose and true happiness. The Bible reminds us in **1 Samuel 15:22** that it is better to be obedient than to offer sacrifices.

> And Samuel said, Hath the LORD *as great* delight in burnt offerings and sacrifices, as in obeying the voice of the LORD? Behold, to obey *is* better than sacrifice, *and* to hearken than the fat of rams.

The joy of obedience is far greater than the pain of sacrifice. Allow God to use your vessel. Maybe your vessel has been broken, but keep in mind that God can use your broken vessel and make it into a blessing to many. The same way He has used mine, He can and will use yours. All you need to do is remain in prayer and be obedient to His call. It is so amazing how God specializes in making nothing into something. God is so good at taking a broken vessel and making that vessel into a work of art for His glory.

God has transformed my life from nothing and made me into a person that seeks to honor Him and offer praise for His glory. He has open doors I never dreamed of. He has taken me places I never imagined going. He has also closed doors, and in the end, He has blessed me beyond measure.

I say this to inspire you. I was a nobody who few people knew about. I was just an old ragged clay and God turned me around. God can and will turn your life around. It doesn't matter how messed up you are; He will turn your mess into a message and your sorrow into song; He will turn your mourning into dancing and your weeping into smiling. I can speak with confidence because He has done it for me. If you remain with Him, He will do it for you.

We spend so much time trying to fix it, but I challenge you to let go and let God take control of your life. Let God be the driving force in your life; allow Him to unleash his divine purpose in you, so you may live a life of true happiness and purpose.

Pause for a moment. Now whisper a prayer and tell God you need to discover your purpose. If you have discovered it but still need direction, ask Him to guide your path so you may live a life that contains true happiness. Ask Him to reveal to you what He needs you to do for His kingdom. Listen for a few minutes and then move on.

When You Pray, Listen, Because God Speaks

God speaks to us in many ways. One way He speaks is through His Word. He uses His prophets, He speaks through our thoughts, He speaks through circumstances. If God is speaking to you now, then make a note of it. Write it down so you will remember.

_____

_____

Develop a Mindset That You Will Live a Life of Purpose

A made-up mind is a purpose-driven mind. Nothing beats a made-up mind. Have you ever just decided to accomplish a task and told yourself that no matter what, you would get it done?

A made-up mind leads to determination, and you need to be determined to fulfill your purpose. You become so focused, you have no room for negative thoughts. All God needs is to get your mind to the place where it is made up—made up to seek after Him, made up to walk in your purpose, and made up to find true happiness.

To find your purpose and walk in true happiness, you must decide to stay with God. If you have not accepted Him as your Lord and Savior, then you must make up your mind right now to let Him come into your heart and transform your life.

In my hometown, we normally sing this little hymn: *Come into my heart, come into my heart, Lord Jesus, come in to stay, come in I pray, come into my heart, Lord Jesus.*

Invite God into your life now. Finding true happiness is all about seeking God. You cannot live a life that will bring you true happiness until you begin to have an encounter with God.

The Bible reminds us of the encounter Jacob had with God. He knew this person he was wrestling with was no ordinary person. During his encounter, Jacob decided not to let the angel of God go until he blessed him. Jacob wrestled with him and when the man saw that he didn't prevail against Jacob, he touched his hip. Jacob's hip was put out of joint as he continued to wrestle with him, "And he said, Thy name shall be called no more Jacob, but Israel: for as a prince hast thou power with God and with men, and hast prevailed." (**Genesis 32:28**).

Prevail and Break Through Into Your Purpose

When did you last wrestle with God? When did you last put aside your comfortable sheets and pillows and stay up all night praying? My desire for you is that you will wrestle with God—wrestle in your prayer, wrestle in your faith, wrestle with a made-up mind to hold on to Him until He blesses you. Let Him change your name, allow Him to rewrite your life, let Him give you a purposeful start—a start that produces joy, peace, and happiness. Develop a made-up mind and move into your divine calling. You were created to be happy; you were created to live a life that produces blessing and happiness. The life that God desires for you is far greater than the one you desire for yourself. Live a life of blessing and favor by fulfilling your purpose here on earth.

Let's Pray:

Heavenly Father, as we present Your child to You, You know the areas in their life that they need to surrender. We pray even now that as they begin to read this prayer, You will give them the strength to surrender and lay it at Your feet. Help them to know that the reward of being obedient is far greater than the giving up of sacrifices. I ask that Your anointing will connect them to You in Spirit so they may live a purposeful life that will lead them to the pathway of finding true happiness while on earth. We give You thanks in Jesus' name. Amen.

CHAPTER 7

Your Attitude Will Determine Your Altitude

Have you ever escaped from the busy world and city lights to drive to the mountains to relax and enjoy the cool breeze and the quietness of mother nature? It is so amazing to look at the mountains—how high the trees are, how they toil not, yet still, they flourish with their green vegetation, and our heavenly Father clothes them. Are you not more than they, ye of little faith? Rejoice in the Lord and rest assured that your labor will not be in vain. As I write this chapter, I imagine you going on this journey to finding your purpose and true happiness, and it gives me hope and great joy, which I know you will experience very soon.

It is so amazing how God has a way of beautifying mother nature. I believe this is so because the trees and birds are obedient to the function that God gives them to carry out. They not only fulfill us by beautifying our surroundings, but they provide the flow of oxygen for us. We cannot see the air we breathe, but we can feel it and see the movement of the trees, and they sway to the winds gushing through their branches. Isn't mother nature beautiful? Mother nature's attitude has determined its altitudes.

As I journeyed through the mountains and as I sat outside watching how tall these trees grow, it dawned on my heart that the attitude of men will determine their altitude in God.

Simply put, your attitude toward God will determine how far God takes you in life. Your attitude can alter your success, or it can add value to your life, allowing you to live a purpose-driven life that leads toward success.

My questions to you are, how is your attitude toward God and the things of God? Are you living a life of obedience? Do you seek to put God first in everything you do?

A life of obedience will allow God to take you to the altitude you need to reach. Have you ever wondered why things are not going the way you desire them to go? Or you just can't seem to move from where you are? Or everything you do just doesn't make sense? Check your attitude toward God and the things of God.

Kevin Downswell, a famous Jamaican Gospel Artist, sings a well-known song titled **"If It's Not You, Then Lord It's Nothing."** This is the kind of attitude God desires for us to have for Him. He wants us to realize that if it's not Him, then it's nothing at all. It's not about your desire, it's not about your job, it's not about your bank account, it's all about Jesus.

King Solomon wrote in **Ecclesiastes 2:11:** "Then I looked on all the works that my hands had wrought, and on the labour that I had laboured to do: and, behold, all *was* vanity and vexation of spirit, and *there was* no profit under the sun."

King Solomon was the richest and wisest man, and he concluded that all he had accomplished in life meant nothing at the end of his journey. It did not bring him great joy and true happiness. Happiness is not found in the things of the world and the things we accomplish. True happiness is found when we begin to live a purpose-driven life that leads to carrying out the will of God. It is found when we become obedient to God's Word and transform our attitude, and our way of living, to be in alignment with His will for our life. Our attitude will determine how much we accomplish in life. Check your attitude and seek to please God in everything you do.

I have realized that I was created for one purpose and that purpose is to carry out the will and the plans that God has for my life. What plans does God have for your life? Do you desire to find out? Do you desire to make your attitude one of obedience to God? Then start to live a purpose-driven life. Purpose brings forth life.

Enduring Suffering

Have you ever stopped and wondered, "Am I enduring suffering because my attitude is not where it should be with God?" Could one's period of suffering mean that God wants you to get your attitude in line with His will for your life?

I now understand that most people wait until they are enduring great affliction and suffering before they surrender their life to God. That's the wrong choice.

> God will not bless you physically until He gets you in alignment with your purpose. Through fulfilling your purpose, you will be blessed. "A man's gift makes room for him, and brings him before great men." (**Proverbs 18:16**).

The longer you take to realize this, the longer you will remain in the stage of confusion, hurt, bitterness, failure, and hopelessness.

In order for you to receive your blessing physically, God must sometimes take you to a place of brokenness. This is what we, most times, call suffering. Have you ever felt as if God has somehow forgotten about you? I have felt it. I have questioned the will of God for my life, being broken to the point of complete surrender. But the olive must go through many stages, so like the olive, you may be broken and battered and beaten, but God is going to pull you through.

We tend to want things our way, which is why the process sometimes take so long. You must first understand that it is not your way.

If we take the time out to truly examine our lives, then we will see that we have so many attitudes to get rid of. It's a process, and with God's help, you will get rid of them.

Change Your Jar

God cannot pour new wine into an old vessel; the new wine will have no taste because the old wine has a stronger flavor. The longer you keep wine, the stronger it becomes. In order for God to do a new work in you, you must be willing to pour out the old wine, so your vessel will be cleansed. You wouldn't pour water or juice into a dirty glass. The mere fact that the glass is dirty will be a huge turn-off. God cannot take you to higher heights until your attitude is in line with His will and purpose for your life.

Develop the Right Attitude

Having the right attitude towards God is a plus. When you get to this point, you now give God the **access** to take you to the altitude He has for your life. Ask Him to create in you a clean heart and renew a right spirit within you. Desire His presence in your life and He will reveal the plans and the purpose He has for you. Tell Him you desire more of Him and less of you.

Spend some time seeking God, by prayer and fasting. I often tell people don't fast for your needs because God already knows your needs before you ask Him. Fast for the renewing of your spirit, the changing of your life (attitude), the will of God to be done in you so your purpose will be birthed. If you develop this attitude, then you will be amazed at the distance God will take you in Him.

Remember, your attitude will determine your altitude. Simply put, your distance in life depends on the attitude you have towards God and the things of God.

Let's Pray:

Heavenly Father, I come to You with the assurance of knowing that anything I ask in Your name shall be done. Even now, Lord, I ask that You transform our attitudes to be in line with the plans and purpose You have for my life. Teach me now, Lord, how to live a life of obedience so I will fulfill the plans and the purpose You have for my life. In Jesus' name, Amen.

CHAPTER 8

Walking In Your Purpose

Purpose is the reason for which something is done or created or for which something exists. I cannot emphasize this meaning enough; I have been intrigued with the importance of living a purpose-driven life.

One word that joins with purpose is connection. Purpose connects you in every way you can think or imagine. It connects you with the will of God, it connects you with the right set of people; purpose gives life meaning. You are about to be connected to the true vine.

John 15:1-5 - I am the true vine, and my Father is the husbandman. Every branch in me that beareth not fruit he taketh away: and every *branch* that beareth fruit, he purgeth it, that it may bring forth more fruit. Now ye are clean through the word which I have spoken unto you. Abide in me, and I in you. As the branch cannot bear fruit of itself, except it abide in the vine; no more can ye, except ye abide in me. I am the vine, ye *are* the branches: He that abideth in me, and I in him, the same bringeth forth much fruit: for without me ye can do nothing.

You cannot live a purpose-driven life unless you are connected to the true vine, which is **Jesus Christ.** Everything that should come from the vine is connected to your divine purpose, the reason for which you were created. Can the one who was created tell the Creator the reason for which they were created? **No.** The true vine knows the reason for which you were created.

Get Connected to the Source

The source is the giver of life. "And the LORD God formed man *of* the dust of the ground, and breathed into his nostrils the breath of life; and man became a living soul." (**Genesis 2:7**).

Man is made up of three parts: the body, the soul, and spirit. The body is known as the physical aspect of mankind or the structure of mankind. The Spirit is known as the non-physical part of a person. This part is said to seat the emotions of an individual (your character). An example of the soul is said to be the part of you that makes you who you are, and that part will live on after you die.

Man was created to live a purpose-driven life. Purpose brings joy, happiness, blessing, and prosperity. Have you ever watched a person who lives a purpose-driven life, how their life just automatically flows by the will and power of God?

What is Your Purpose?

You must get to the point in your life where you begin to seek your purpose. You must reach a place where you ask God the question,

"Why was I created? What purpose was I created to carry out? What plans do You have for my life?"

The plans you have for your life may not always be the will of God for your life. The will of God is different from your physical plans. Many times in Scripture Jesus stated that His will was to carry out the plans of the One who sent Him. **John 6:38:** "For I came down from heaven, not to do mine own will, but the will of him that sent me."

Now, what was the will of Him who sent Jesus?

And he said unto them, How is it that ye sought me? wist ye not that I must be about my Father's business? (**Luke 2:49**).

This text shows us that Jesus had gone off to do the will of His Father. His earthly parents searched for Him. When they found Him, she questioned Jesus, and He responded with that statement. What could be so fascinating about His Father's will? Why was He so eager to do it?

Jesus understood that the will of His Father was greater than His desire. He knew that God had sent Him into this world to accomplish one purpose, and no matter what, He had to fulfill that ultimate plan and purpose.

Each of us was sent to this world to carry out an ultimate purpose, and that is to make disciples of men. While Jesus was on earth, His purpose was to die for you and me, and in so doing, He set up His Father's kingdom here on earth, so we could carry out His ultimate plan and purpose for our lives.

Jesus gave His disciple a command—to go and make disciples of men.

"Go ye therefore, and teach all nations, baptizing them in the name of the Father, and of the Son, and of the Holy Ghost:" (**Mathew 28:19**).

We were all created to carry out this purpose and to glorify our heavenly Father (See also **Psalm 19:1**).

Each person was given this one ultimatum, but in this ultimate purpose, each person was given a different assignment. The challenge now is to discover your assignment. What is God's plan for your life? What are the steps God has created for you to carry out these functions? The steps are in your divine calling, your assignment; it is your purpose.

Your Soul Connects Your Purpose

We were all created with a soul that gives life. Your soul was given an assignment to complete. In this assignment, God places your soul inside a body made from dust. He gives the body emotions to carry out through the function of your spirit. This assignment is your purpose.

You were created to live a purpose-driven life. Life becomes meaningless and unhappy when you are not operating in the function you were designed to carry out. You cannot be happy and at peace until you begin to carry out this assignment that was given to you before the foundations of the earth.

How Can I Fulfill My Purpose?

Get connected to the source:

Everything will come from here:

1. **Everything is connected to the Source**: John 15:5 says He is the true vine. He alone can allow you to bear fruit.

2. **You must allow the Source to feed you**: You cannot fulfill your purpose unless you are connected to the source. A person connected to the source lives a life full of favor because they will carry out the plans and the purpose that the Source has created them to do. Picture the Source—like electricity, only it can generate light. Only from the Source will life come. A person living in darkness will never be truly happy; they will never see the light. Light allows one to see and be at peace. The Source will birth your purpose, and you will generate life.

3. **Stay plugged into your Source**: The moment you get disconnected from the Source, all life will be taken from you. You cannot carry out or live a purpose-driven life unless you are connected. Connection brings forth power and dominion to operate by the master's plans. A powerless person is a defeated person.

4. **Consult your Source**: Never make a decision, no matter how small it is, unless you consult the Source. Remember, the Source is the One who created you. You were created to carry out His function. He knows the path He has designed to get you there.

5. **Get the Source involved**: Seek to develop an intimate relationship with the Source. Through this relationship, you will form a bond; the bond will open up communication; communication will bring forth clarity, trust, love, assurance, hope, fulfillment, and your purpose. Get to know the Source.

6. **Make a sacrifice for the Source**: Give up anything that will disconnect you from the Source. Remember, only in the Source can you find life. Without life, you cannot live a purpose-driven life. You must find time to be with your Source. Any unhealthy relationship, give it up; any form of temptation, cut it loose. Staying connected to your Source is far more important.

7. **Love your Source**: Above all, seek to love God. He is your Source.

Trust Your Source

Trust God. You won't know why you were created until God reveals it to you. God will not give you every detail of your life. You must leave room for your faith to grow. Your faith grows when you begin to trust and obey the Word of God.

God will reveal your purpose to you, and He will show you the way to walk in it. Sometimes He won't reveal to you what is in the middle; sometimes He allows the middle to be so dark and you start to question your purpose. But during this time, you must seek to hold on to the words of God. His Word contains life and power. Remember, He is the source.

When you become fearful in your purpose, trust God to replace fear with faith. Fear cripples your mind and hinders you from trusting God. Fear tells you, "No. Stop. You cannot do this. You will fail. You will be disappointed," but Faith tells you, "Hey, God has got you covered. Remember, you are connected to the true Vine and only in me you will find life." Use your faith to conquer your fear.

Your Purpose is Bigger Than Your Fear

Allow your purpose to give you your vision. Write down your vision below and put a value on it. Each time you think about giving up, go back to your vision.

_____

_____

_____

_____

What does your vision mean to you?

_____

_____

_____

_____

Why is it so important for you to accomplish your vision?

_____

_____

_____

_____

Proverbs 29:18 says: Where *there is* no vision, the people perish: but he that keepeth the law, happy *is* he.

You need your vision. There is no secret to fulfilling your purpose. Just give yourself to God so He can use you for His glory.

A made-up mind is a mind that beats the odds, the odds of 'I can't,' the odds of disappointment, the odds of rejection, and the odds of failure.

There is no failure in purpose. You cannot fail, you will not fail, don't allow fear to make you believe you can fail. Remember, you were created to carry this out. Once you are connected to the true Vine, your purpose will be fulfilled.

Purpose cannot die. The mere fact that you are alive means you have not completed your purpose. Don't be fearful of death. Purpose is in you; life is inside of you waiting to be unleashed.

Let's Pray:

Heavenly Father, we come to You today knowing that many are the plans in a man's heart, but it is Your plans and purpose that will prevail. Teach me, Lord, how to walk in Your purpose so that Your will for my life will come to pass. In Jesus' name. Amen.

CHAPTER 9

Be Still and Know That He Is God

Be still, and know that I *am* God: I will be exalted among the heathen, I will be exalted in the earth. (**Psalm 46:10).**

Oftentimes we get so discouraged and caught up in today's society. Our emotions weigh us down; past hurt, pain, and fear of tomorrow tend to form strongholds in our lives. But the secret to living a life of purpose that leads to true happiness is to remember that God is in control right now.

Nothing can take God by surprise. I want you to formulate a picture of a situation in your mind that you are currently battling or facing. Now write it down.

_____

_____

_____

_____

_____

_____

_____

_____

Ask yourself the question, "Did this take God by surprise?" The answer is **No**. He is the all-wise God, He is all knowing, and He is ever-present; in short, He is omnipotent, omniscient, and omnipresent.

If God is the one who created you, then He knows the reason He is allowing you to go through this period. Look back at what you have written down. Now instead of asking God, "Why me?" ask Him what He wants you to learn from this situation. There is a lesson to learn from every situation we go through. What weighs us down is that we tend to complain and get angry at God, and by doing so, we miss the bigger and greater picture of what God wants us to gain from it.

Do Not Complain

Complaining gets us nowhere. All it does is rob us of our peace of mind, joy, and happiness. It makes us bitter and angry, which leads to us not appreciating the blessings God has in store for us. The Bible reminds us in **1 Thessalonians 5:18** – "In every thing give thanks: for this is the will of God in Christ Jesus concerning you."

This is a powerful verse. Can you give thanks when you are on your death bed and the doctors say you will not recover? Can you give thanks when cancer takes away your loved ones? Can you give thanks when the bills are due, and they are about to foreclose on your home? Can you give thanks when life seems to be weighing you down? Can you give thanks when your plans are not coming through? It's a tough one, if we are to be truthful.

But yes, we should give thanks because it is the perfect will of God for our life through Christ Jesus. I have prayed and asked God these questions: Why me? Why me, Lord? Why all the pain, the rejection, the hurt, the confusion? Why does everything seem to be going wrong? For years I asked myself these questions over and over, until I attended a church seminar and the preacher called me out from my seat and he began to prophetically speak over my life. He frankly said, "You have been constantly asking God why you. God says to tell you, Yes, it is you; it has to be you." Hearing this, tears fell from my eyes.

Every situation you have gone through, and will go through, will help shape you into becoming the person God has created you to be. Your pain is not in vain. There is purpose in your pain. Don't fight the pain; allow the pain to birth your purpose.

How can I allow the pain to birth my purpose?

Stop complaining: Ask God to carry you through. When God takes you through the circumstances, allow Him to prepare you physically and spiritually. Going through the situation will mold you and teach you. The painful situations will become a great testimony when you have unleashed your divine purpose. Your pain will give you strength. You will no longer be weak, but you become strong in Christ Jesus.

We all need a testimony and only through our pain will we be able to get our breakthrough. **God has got you covered.**

Pain produces a plan. A plan brings forth purpose. When we allow God to use our pain to shape our purpose, then God's plans for our life will come into place. God has a plan for your life, and His plan is greater than the ones we have for ourselves. How can we make plans for ourselves when we were not created by ourselves? We must first seek to know and establish the plans that the Creator has for our lives.

>   **Isaiah 43:7:** *Even* every one that is called by my name: for I have created him for my glory, I have formed him; yea, I have made him.

>   **Ephesians 1:11:** In whom also we have obtained an inheritance, being predestinated according to the purpose of him who worketh all things after the counsel of his own will:

>   **Ephesians 2:10**: For we are his workmanship, created in Christ Jesus unto good works, which God hath before ordained that we should walk in them.

We are His handiwork. His creation. His achievement. His design.

We belong to God. God owns us; He is the Creator.

God had a plan in mind when He created you.

Mirror Challenge

Look at yourself in the mirror and repeat **Ephesians 1:11**: In whom also we have obtained an inheritance, being predestinated according to the purpose of him who worketh all things after the counsel of his own will.

Insert your name: I _____ was chosen. I was selected as the best. Out of the millions of sperm that were released, God chose me. It is not the fact that I reached the egg first. **No**, it is because God chose me; He had a plan in mind when He allowed me to reach the egg first. I was born a winner. It is in my DNA to win. The fact that I was born a winner means God has equipped and empowered me for the season I am in. I am not a mistake. I will not allow fear and depression and self-guilt to weigh me down. I will arise and take up my rightful position in the Kingdom of God. I will let my purpose create the way for my destiny and true happiness in my life.

Your Life is Worth Living

God has chosen you, He has predestined you. 'Pre' means before – 'destined' means a pre-planned fate. Don't consider your life ordinary. You were not created to be ordinary; you were given an assignment to carry out. God has invested in your greatness, and you must bring this assignment to pass by walking in your purpose. Before you were created, God pre-planned your life. He has an assignment already planned out for you to accomplish. You cannot leave this earth and not bring to pass this assignment. Your purpose is what you were created to carry out.

He Had Me In His Plans

A few years ago, while I was yet still a sinner, I dreamed I was walking down an alley and encountered two men. One of the men said, "You are going to die." I was terrified of death because I really didn't understand that purpose cannot die. In the dream, I began to cry. Suddenly, a paper fell from heaven into my hand. When I looked at the paper, a great sense of joy and peace flooded my soul. I was given the hope and assurance that something great was in store for me. I boldly turned to the men and said, "No, I will not die. Here is a list of all the great things God has for me to carry out on earth." I did not understand then what my plan and purpose was. I knew I saw a long list written with the assignment God wanted me to carry out. Little did I know God had me in mind.

You Are In His Plans

God had you in His plan even before you were formed in your mother's womb (See **Jeremiah 1:5**).

God has an assignment for you with your name written on it. Until your life gets in alignment with His will, you will not fulfill your purpose. Everything you hope for or dream of is connected to your purpose. Find your purpose and you will find true happiness.

His Plans

God has a plan for you. In this plan is your divine purpose waiting for you to carry it out. This purpose has a master blueprint with your assignment written on it. They were not your plans, so you will not fail.

It is not your work. We are just the vessels God chose to use so His work will come to pass once we surrender our lives to Him.

It is His work, His doing. You cannot carry out the plans yourself, and you must go back to the Creator, so He can bring to pass His purpose in your life. When we begin to understand the work of God in the lives of His people, then surrendering becomes easier. We don't belong to ourselves; we belong to God, so everything must come from Him, who is our source. He will work everything according to your conformity with the purpose of his will.

Key Notes

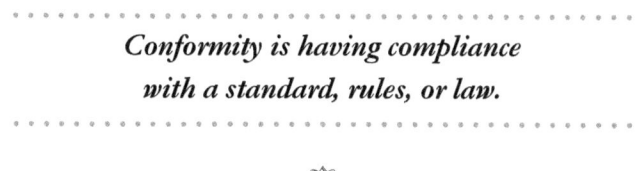

Conformity is having compliance with a standard, rules, or law.

God is saying "I have given you some rules, standards, and regulations to govern you while you are carrying out the assignment I have given you. Once you abide in My words and let My word abide in you, I will bring to pass the plans and the purpose I have for your life" **(See John 15:7)**.

Living a purpose-driven life is not as hard as we may think. When you begin to live a life pleasing to God, you will see His will in a new light.

> *You were not created to do everything. The quicker you get this, the easier it will be for you. You cannot do everything; you cannot be everybody.*

God created you unique. He has given you special traits. Only you can fulfill your purpose; don't try to be everyone. Find 'you' and be you. You were created to fulfill the plans that God has for your life.

We worry, get depressed, and become unhappy because we are not living a purpose-driven life. Your soul understands the reason for which it was created. Once you are not carrying out that purpose, then there will always be a fight going on between the soul and the flesh. Begin to live a purpose-driven life and allow the Word of God to come to life inside your body. Remember, purpose is the reason you were created. Find your purpose and find the pathway to true happiness.

In the beginning, Adam and Eve were created with one purpose and that was to worship God. They didn't work, yet the trees would take care of themselves; the animals would be fed; there was no rain; the rivers never ran dry, and everything was beautiful upon the face of the earth. We struggle to make it in life because our lives are not in line with the will of God. When your life begins to be in alignment to the will of God, then God will take care of your needs, and all you need to do is serve Him, worship Him, be obedient to His Word, and allow Him to carry out His purpose in your life. Relax and allow God to do His work in your life. Seek to find your purpose and be truly happy.

> *Let's Pray:*
>
> *Heavenly Father, may you reign inside me, so I will be in alignment with my purpose and my steps on earth will be directed by You. In Jesus' name. Amen.*

CHAPTER 10

Reposition Your Life to the Will of God

We have come to the shift, the middle of the Pathway to finding Purpose and True Happiness. Repositioning of oneself is so important in the journey to living a purpose-driven life. You must decide to reposition yourself to carry out your God-ordained purpose and live a life of happiness. In doing this, you will be broken, you will feel lonely, you may endure hardship, you may feel hurt, you may be left in the dark, and you may even be left standing alone. Why? Because this is your journey and not everyone may understand it. Only you, with God's help, can go through it. Nobody can change you; nobody can reposition you. There are some things in life that only you can do for yourself, and this is one of them.

The change must take place. You must desire this shift; you must begin to see, feel, and taste purpose; you must envision it; begin to live it in your mind. Once you start to unclothe your purpose by living it in the mind, the universe will respond to your command. God has invested in you something known as the power of the spoken word. Your words contain life, power, and authority; use them to transform your life.

"Have not I commanded thee? Be strong and of a good courage; be not afraid, neither be thou dismayed: for the LORD thy God *is* with thee whithersoever thou goest." **(Joshua 1:9).**

The Lord is on your side. I speak a shift in your life. I speak strength, I speak boldness, I speak courage, I send forth the faith needed for you to believe in yourself and live a purpose-driven life. May you begin to use your words to birth your purpose and to shift into God's favor.

Your words contain life: "Then spake Joshua to the LORD in the day when the LORD delivered up the Amorites before the children of Israel, and he said in the sight of Israel, Sun, stand thou still upon Gibeon; and thou, Moon, in the valley of Ajalon" **(Joshua 10:12).**

Joshua was a man just like you, and what made him extraordinary was his faith and belief in the God he serves. He had faith in his God. He knew that God had a purpose for his life, and in that purpose, God gave him authority.

What is keeping you from embracing your purpose?

Faith is developed—faith is grown. If you desire your faith to grow, believe everything that the Word of God says and put it into practice.

Take A Stand

Somethings must be left behind. You must decide to leave some people behind. At some point, you must decide to **stand alone**. You cannot change the universe until you change yourself.

The Change Must Begin With You

Don't try to be everyone; you cannot carry everyone's burden until you have repositioned yourself. Picture a broken glass; can you drink from a broken glass? **No**. You must first mend the broken glass before you can drink from it. A broken heart cannot give love. If you are broken, you cannot love your spouse, you cannot love your children, you cannot love your friends. A broken person tends to push people aside. They will let you in, but there is a wall that blocks them from giving you full access.

Break the wall: Give Jesus your heart so He can mend it for you. Feeling sad, tired, confused, depressed, hurt, or heartbroken? God is saying, give Me your mind and let Me take you on a quick conquest. Block out all distractions; give me your full attention. Now inhale and exhale. Cry if you must; allow your heart to experience whatever you are currently going through. Don't hold it back; allow the feeling to consume you.

While it is consuming you, give your mind to God. Begin to activate the power of the spoken word. Command your feelings to **stand still** under the authority of the **Holy Spirit**. Speak to the feelings and let them know who is in control.

Speak to your mind: *I am purpose driven, I was created to carry out God's plans for my life, I was given authority to bring every thought not in line with the Word of God under subjection.*

Begin to demolish the ungodly, negative thoughts and feelings.

> **2 Corinthians 10:5:** Casting down imaginations, and every high thing that exalteth itself against the knowledge of God, and bringing into captivity every thought to the obedience of Christ.

I demolish arguments and every pretension that sets itself up against the knowledge of God, and I take captive every thought to make it obedient to Christ. **Hold on to the power of the spoken word.**

Shift Your Mindset

Have you ever noticed how runners position themselves? The moment they are called to the marking line, everything around them is shut down. They are in the world, but their mind is only in one place—to reach the finish line first.

Where is your mindset?

What are you envisioning?

What position are you taking to bring your dreams, visions, and purpose to life?

What difference are you making?

What are you eliminating from your daily routine?

What sacrifices are you willing to make to fulfill your purpose?

You must make a change; you must start somewhere.

Repositioning begins in the mind. *What are the thoughts that keep surfacing in your mind?*

What movies are you watching?

What songs are you listening to?

What books are you reading?

What friends are you hanging out with?

Who are you dating?

Everything must begin with a shift. You cannot live a life of victory and still hold on to the same old hobbies. You must first come to a state of mind where you say to yourself, "I am not pleased with the life I am living." Even if you are, you must go to a higher level in Christ.

The Bible reminds us that He offers us new mercies every day. "They are new every morning: great is your faithfulness" (**Lamentations 3:23**). It means every day you are alive, God has something new prepared for you.

Are you willing to change? Are you ready to receive it? How often do you envision your shift? How badly do you desire it? If you have decided to walk in your purpose and find true happiness, then begin to find your purpose and live a life of true happiness.

Let's Pray:

Father, we come to You in the name of Your son Jesus Christ. We command everything working against Your children to be shifted by the power and authority of Your Holy Spirit. Transform their mindset to Your perfect will in Christ Jesus. We pray that their plans will become Your will for their life. We speak to every fear that is tormenting their minds, and we release the power of faith. We declare that they will arise and take up their rightful position in the kingdom of heaven, so they will walk in the purpose and live the life You have created for them. Open doors and align their footsteps to meet Your plans for their life. Amen.

CHAPTER 11

The Beauty of Trusting God

At some point in our lives, we have heard about trusting in God, how to trust in God, why it is important to trust in God, and the list goes on. Trusting in God takes the form of obedience. You cannot trust God until you have reached the point of living an obedient life.

This is more than just talking the talk—this is walking the walk. There is no talk in this. This life contains self-denial, moments of fear, moments of second-guessing yourself, moments of wondering, 'Is it me speaking or is it God?' Moments when you become so scared, you question your own ability to rise.

As I examined my life, I knew deep inside it was time to unleash my divine purpose. At that point, I had to be willing to let go of the *Sherdeine* I knew to become the Sherdeine God had created me to be.

This brought a moment of fear as reality rushed through my mind and thoughts. The reality of becoming humble even to the point of death, the reality of not being able to fight my own battles, the reality of not being able to retaliate and take matters into my own hands. The thoughts were all about me. Then the Holy Spirit brought to my mind: It is never about you, it will never be about you, you are just the vessel I have created and have chosen to use.

He said, "It is now time to remove self, so I can place My Spirit in you, so My purpose will be accomplished through you."

You Must Decrease, So God Can Increase

The moment you begin to see through the eyes of God, then you will decrease. "He must increase, but I *must* decrease" **(John 3:30).**

You must decrease so that God's Spirit can become greater in you, for your life is not your own. You belong to God. Paul stated: "To the weak became I as weak, that I might gain the weak: I am made all things to all *men*, that I might by all means save some." **(1 Corinthians 9:22).** A life of trust allows you to become humble even unto death. Jesus lived a life of trust and obedience to God. He gave up all power and became humble, even unto death, for His purpose to be accomplished.

What do you need to do to accomplish your purpose?

Living a purpose-driven life has taught me to live a life of obedience and trust, even to the point of becoming submissive to the One who created me. This was all so frightening to me because we were created as beings with willpower. As previously stated, one of the hardest things for us to give up is control. Living a life of trusting God means you will have to give up control, you cannot live for yourself, you must become immune to your own will.

Jesus felt every pain; the disciples felt every pain, but they had to become immune in order to accomplish the greater good. If they had given in to their own feelings and not trusted in God, they would not have accomplished the purpose they were created for.

You Must Give Up To Gain

Trusting in God means giving up. You must reach a place in your walk where you give up on the life you feel comfortable with, to gain the life you were created for. You must allow Him to take care of you.

Mathew 7:7-11 - Ask, and it will be given to you; seek, and you will find; knock, and it will be opened to you. For everyone who asks receives, and he who seeks finds, and to him who knocks it will be opened. Or what man is there among you who, when his son asks for a loaf, will give him a stone? Or if he asks for a fish, he will not give him a snake, will he? If you then, being evil, know how to give good gifts to your children, how much more will your Father who is in heaven give what is good to those who ask Him!

Trusting In God Brings Inner Peace

Have you desired to experience the peace that surpasses all human understanding? I do. Don't feel alone. We are all a work in progress; we all have room for improvement.

"And the peace of God, which passeth all understanding, shall keep your hearts and minds through Christ Jesus" (**Philippians 4:7**). This peace can only be accomplished one way—by living a life of trust in, and obedience to God.

Are you at a point in your life where you feel afraid of letting go and trusting God?

Have you let go, but still struggle to trust God?

You are not alone. We have all been at this point in our life, where the fear of stepping out into the unknown makes us feel paralyzed, but I am reminded each day of the plans and the purpose God has for my life. I'm reminded that the universe needs me. I was created to impact and bring about changes in the universe. I was created to transform and leave my footprint in the universe.

You are a child of the universe. You were created for the universe, which exists because God had you in His plan. You are a child of purpose, and your purpose is bigger than your fear.

You were created for His purpose. Your purpose existed even before you were created. You were created to carry out the plans in the universe, these plans are floating around waiting for you to walk in your purpose.

You cannot die and leave this world without experiencing the life you were created to live. Do not allow the enemy to rob you of this amazing life that God has already predestined for you to carry out. Live a life that contains power, live a life of trust, live a life driven by purpose, live a life that leads to finding true happiness.

This book is entitled *The Pathway to Finding Purpose and True Happiness* because the way is already created for you. All you need to do is find the path that leads to your purpose and you will automatically find true happiness.

And in very deed for this *cause* have I raised thee up, for to shew *in* thee my power; and that my name may be declared throughout all the earth. (**Exodus 9:16**).

Your purpose was created for you. You were created for one reason—to fulfill the purpose God has predestined for you, so His name will be glorified in the earth.

Purpose Cannot Fail

For many years, the enemy made me feel like a failure, a reject, a person living without hope. I questioned the reason for my existence, trying to find a place in the world where I fit in, trying to please everybody except myself.

These feelings are all the plans of the enemy to make you feel unwanted. He knows that if you ever discover your purpose and understand who you are in Christ, then you will become unstoppable; he will no longer have any say and control over your life. Living a life of trust and obedience will allow God to build a hedge of protection around you, your family, your home; even your friends will receive the blessings that will be poured over your life.

I dare you to find your purpose.
I double dare you to walk in your purpose.
I triple dare you to trust God.

The secret is to trust in God and defeat the plans of the enemy over your life. Don't allow the enemy to steal your joy and hinder you from walking in your purpose.

The enemy is afraid of the child of God who lives a purpose-driven life. Why? You are no longer living for yourself, but you begin to live for God. When you live for God, He will honor His Word.

We are reminded by His Word: For the LORD God *is* a sun and shield: the LORD will give grace and glory: no good *thing* will he withhold from them that walk uprightly (**Psalm 84:11**).

Every good thing you desire is connected to living a purpose-driven life.

Let's Pray:

Heavenly Father, we ask that You keep us connected so we will reap the fruits of Your blessing, knowing that no good thing will You withhold from me if I walk upright with You. In Jesus' name. Amen.

CHAPTER 12

Living A Life of Blessings and Miracles

Psalm 37:23-24: The steps of a good **man are ordered by the LORD**: and he delighteth in his way. Though he falls, he shall not be utterly cast down: for the **LORD** upholdeth him with his hand.

Welcome to walking in your blessing and miracles. It's already done.

Man's Rejection is God's Appointment

There are many times in our lives when we are rejected by our loved ones. We have endured broken hearts, we have suffered pain, we have cried tears, we have felt hurt, our hearts have been broken and shattered into pieces by the ones we thought would never let us down. We have loved beyond our own ability and understanding, and we have given our bodies to be used and abused by men, only to be rejected in the end.

Maybe you are hurting now, maybe you have just overcome a broken heart, maybe you are experiencing failure. Cry if you must. It is okay to feel rejected; it is okay to feel hurt, but it is not okay to give up. It is not okay to give in, it is not okay to quit. Yes, you are feeling tired; yes, your strength is failing; yes, you have done everything **humanly possible**. Underline **humanly possible,** because there is a difference. What seems impossible with men, is possible with God. Yes, you have heard this time and time again; you have even read it before. But have you started to live it? Have you started to use it to transform your mind?

Many Bible characters were rejected by men. One of my favorite characters is Joseph. He was rejected by his brothers. They hated him because of the purpose on his life.

God will allow men to reject you, so your purpose will be birthed. Joseph had to be rejected and sold and thrown into the pit and placed in the prison to reach his purpose (Palace).

If you are rejected in any way, whether by your family, friends, loved ones, job loss, needing healing, or needing a breakthrough, God is getting ready to appoint you for His purpose.

You Will Be Rejected In Order To Be Appointed

I, too, was rejected and hurt by failed relationships. Don't count it all lost when things don't work out as you plan. It may just be God setting you up for his appointment. I too was rejected to be appointed. Why? Because God had an ultimate plan and purpose for my life, and now I can rejoice. You will rejoice too because your purpose is **mightier** than your **rejection**.

Rejections lead you to the throne room of grace broken. It breaks you so God can mold you.

What do you need to accomplish? Let your rejection appoint you. My rejection appointed me for my purpose, and now I am complete in Him who created me to carry out His purpose. You can be complete too, and you will.

Rejection Leads To A Life Of Miracles And Blessings

Rejection connects you to God's ultimate plans and purpose for your life. Joseph's rejection allowed him to reach the palace. God used him to feed His people—the same brothers who threw him in the pit and sold him to the Egyptians to become a slave. God knew that if he didn't allow Joseph to go through this experience, then His plan and purpose would not be possible. The path of rejection you might be facing may just be God appointing you to His throne. God will take your rejection and transform it for His glory, if you allow Him.

Fear holds you back. Fear tells you to hold on to the hurt and pain you feel because fear desires that you live a life of defeat that suppresses your mind and leads to depression. It is fear's desire that you constantly be visiting the doctors, spending all you have trying to cure a diagnosis that cannot be healed by medication. Medication cannot cure depression; they suppress the symptoms by keeping it under control.

Faith releases you into a life of miracles, blessing, and favor. Faith connects you with the plans and purpose God has for your life. Faith heals your mind, heart, body, and soul. Faith cures depression and reminds you that by His stripes you have been healed. Yes! I said you have been healed because you must first believe it in your mind before it can be released in your body. Place your mind on the Word of God, which gives hope and life. I will never advise you to stop consulting your doctors or stop taking your medication. But I recommend that you combine your medication with your faith in God and allow Him to give you complete healing. Choose faith over fear so you can live a life of miracles and blessings.

Allow God to use your rejection to bring you into your miracles and blessings.

Have you been praying for a miracle?

Do you desire His blessing? Turn to God. He knows the reason you were created. And He knows why He allows you to be rejected for His glory.

> *Let's Pray:*
>
> *Heavenly Father, I ask that You take my rejection and appoint me to Your throne. Grant me peace of mind and a heart to trust Your will for my life. In Jesus' name. Amen.*

CHAPTER 13

What Awaits a Life of Purpose and True Happiness?

The beauty that awaits a life driven by purpose and happiness is far beyond human feelings and understanding. This beauty can only be experienced. You must choose to live this life for yourself to understand the experience.

We have heard many people speak solidly about living a life pleasing to God. We have also heard many sermons about the favors and blessing that lie beyond living this walk called faith.

We can only accomplish a purpose-driven life if we choose to be obedient to the will of God and take the walk to experience His power at work in us.

His Power Works Through Us

> **Philippians 2:13:** For it is God which worketh in you both to will and to do of *his* good pleasure.

Experience The Walk

Have you ever wondered why the Bible encourages us to walk by faith and not by sight? Have you ever examined that passage of Scripture? I have heard this verse over and over, spoken about it on numerous occasions, and ministered on it.

But, one day, as I paused to meditate on the plans and the purpose that God has for my life, somehow the Spirit of God brought this passage to mind, **"for we walk by faith, not by sight" (See 2 Corinthians 5:7).**

He gently led me to examine this verse.
Let me walk you through it:

We walk: One of the keywords in the verse is the word **walk.** We understand that walk is an action verb, meaning it takes movement. If we look at the meaning of walk, we will notice that some form of movement will take place. No wonder Jesus did not instruct us to sit by faith.

When it comes to faith in action, we must make some form of movement.

What do you hope to accomplish this month, this year, and this season?

Make a note of it below:

_____
_____
_____
_____

In order for your faith to work, you must move, you must take a step, action must be seen. You cannot experience what awaits a purpose-driven life, if you do not put purpose into action. Faith must be worked; you must take a step.

I challenge you, purpose in your heart, to make a move on your vision so you can experience the life that awaits a walk of purpose.

Testimony

I write this testimony with a smile on my face. This book is all about me putting faith to work. It was written upon a promise from God. If we choose to hold on to God's promises, then He will give to us the power of His manifestation. Faith in action produces God's promises for your life.

Many scriptures in the Bible speak about God's promises for our life. One of my favorite promises can be found in **Jeremiah 29:11**: "For I know the thoughts that I think toward you, saith the LORD, thoughts of peace, and not of evil, to give you an expected end."

This promise reminds me daily that God has a plan for my life. Not only does it tell us there is a plan for our lives, He also tells us of the plan; to prosper us.

God's plan for your life is that you will prosper in whatever stage you are at right now. There is room for prosperity; whether spiritual, emotional, financial, or physical. Whatever stage it is, God's desire for you is to prosper. At this very moment, I want you to pause and repeat over your life that God desires you to prosper in all areas of your life. Now believe it by faith.

The enemy's plan is to make us feel down and forsaken and make us feel that God doesn't want us to live a prosperous life. But God does want us to prosper as our soul prospers. We are reminded to "be ye stedfast, unmoveable, always abounding in the work of the Lord, forasmuch as ye know that your labour is not in vain in the Lord" (**1 Corinthians 15:58**).

For when we labor in God, His plans of a great future for our life will come to pass. There is hope and God gives us this hope. Rest in the assurance of God and in His promises for your life.

God's Promises Bring Forth Protection

Psalm 91:11: For he shall give his angels charge over thee, to keep thee in all thy ways.

When we wait on the promises of God, we don't need to worry about anything.

What are you concerned about? Is it your future? Is it your family? Is it your health? Is it your protection?

May I remind you to "Fear not: for they that *be* with us *are* more than they that *be* with them" (**2 Kings 6:16**). The angels of God encamp around and about those who fear him. The fear of the Lord is to reverence Him, acknowledge Him as Lord and Savior of your life, worship and exalt His name so He will be glorified through you.

The second phrase to examine from the Scripture is **by Faith.**

Let's examine the word **'by.'** According to the English language, it is a **preposition** that identifies the agent performing an action. It also indicates the means of achieving something.

Look closely. We achieve our purpose/visions by **faith.** We know according to **Hebrews 11:1** that "faith is the substance of things hoped for, the evidence of things not seen."

We are told to **walk** (make a move, take action**) by** (perform the action, don't sit) **faith** (make your vision come to pass).

Do not simply wait until you see the evidence of your visions and dreams to act upon them. Instead, move by faith and allow God to bring them to pass. Begin to act and move by working your faith.

> **James 2:14:** What *doth it* profit, my brethren, though a man say he hath faith, and have not works? can faith save him?

Ponder this passage and then make your move toward experiencing a purpose-driven life.

What awaits a purpose-driven life is the manifestation of the Holy Spirit.

True purpose can only be birthed by the **manifestation** of the Holy Spirit. To experience the blessing that awaits a purpose-driven life, one must allow the Holy Spirit to manifest the presence of God in their life.

Let's examine **John 15:5:** I am the vine, ye *are* the branches: He that abideth in me, and I in him, the same bringeth forth much fruit: for without me ye can do nothing.

Manifestation must begin with the vine. There is no shortcut. True purpose and happiness can only be manifested if we are willing to be connected to the vine, which is **Jesus Christ**. Only by Him and through Him will we be able to bear fruit. Whatever good we desire for our life is part of the fruit—the plans, the dreams, the accomplishments, the purpose, the hearts we will be used to bless—everything that God has planned for our lives can only be given to us by **Jesus**. *Apart from Him, you and I can do nothing.*

What are the desires that concern you for your life?

What are the visions that God has revealed to you so far?

Get connected to Jesus. Remain in Him and allow Him to manifest the presence of the Holy Spirit in you. I assure you, you will experience the manifestation of the Holy Spirit. *His Holy Spirit will be manifested in you.*

> **John 16:13:** Howbeit when he, the Spirit of truth, is come, he will guide you into all truth: for he shall not speak of himself; but whatsoever he shall hear, *that* shall he speak: and he will shew you things to come.

His Manifestation Produces Power

If there is one thing all human beings desire to have is power. When God created the world, He gave us dominion and rulership over the things He created (See **Genesis 1:28)**. True power comes only from the manifestation of the Holy Spirit.

John 14:12: Verily, verily, I say unto you, He that believeth on me, the works that I do shall he do also; and greater *works* than these shall he do; because I go unto my Father.

The desire we hope to accomplish can and will be possible when we believe in Jesus and do what He commands.

What did Jesus command?

Matthew 22:37-40: Jesus said unto him, **Thou shalt love** the Lord thy God with all thy heart, and with all thy soul, and with all thy mind. This is the first and great commandment. And the second is like unto it, **Thou shalt love** thy neighbour as thyself. On these two commandments **hang** all the law and the prophets.

If we practice these two commandments of Jesus Christ, then experiencing a purpose-driven life that leads to true happiness will become easier.

1 Peter 4:8: And above all things have fervent charity among yourselves: for charity shall cover the multitude of sins.

God's spirit cannot manifest where there is envy, hatred, or strife. We must abound in love, so the Spirit of God can be manifested in us, so our purpose will be birthed. When purpose is birthed, the manifestation of the Holy Spirit comes to life in us and we will experience what awaits the life driven by purpose and true happiness.

There are blessings that come through the manifestation of the Holy Spirit:

1. **The power of Jesus Christ will be awakened in your life**. Jesus replied, "Jesus answered and said unto him, If a man love me, he will keep my words: and my Father will love him, and we will come unto him, and make our abode with him" **(John 14:23)**. When God abides in us, then all things become possible. Whatever you ask in His name, He will do.

2. **It births God's purpose and plans for our lives:** The LORD of hosts hath sworn, saying, Surely as I have thought, so shall it come to pass; and as I have purposed, *so* shall it stand: **(Isaiah 14:24). God's purpose in your life will stand.**

3. **It gives us authority**: Verily I say unto you, Whatsoever ye shall bind on earth shall be bound in heaven: and whatsoever ye shall loose on earth shall be loosed in heaven. **(Matthew 18:18)**.

Everything that awaits a life of purpose and happiness will be achieved when we allow the Spirit of God to manifest in our lives.

Let's Pray:

Heavenly Father, we come to You in the name of Your Son Jesus Christ. We humbly ask that You manifest Your Spirit inside of us so we can experience the life of joy, peace, favor, and blessings that await a purpose-driven life of happiness. May You continuously work on us so Your Spirit will be evident in our lives. Amen.

CHAPTER 14

Remain In The Waiting Period of God's Timing

Wait on the LORD: be of good courage, and he shall strengthen thine heart: wait, I say, on the LORD. **(Psalm 27:14).**

The waiting period is never the easiest time in our life. It's a period of discomfort, loneliness, and darkness. It's sometimes a season of pain and hurt. During this season, you may feel alone and forsaken to the point where you feel God has forgotten about you.

I called it a season because this period was not meant to stay forever. Even though it may seem long and unbearable, this season too will pass. Seasons are part of nature; seasons are part of our life. The Bible reminds us in **Ecclesiastes 3:1-8: "**To everything there is a season, and a time to every purpose under the heaven: A time to be born, and a time to die; a time to plant, and a time to pluck up that which is planted; A time to kill, and a time to heal; a time to break down, and a time to build up; A time to weep, and a time to laugh; a time to mourn, and a time to dance; A time to cast away stones, and a time to gather stones together; a time to embrace, and a time to refrain from embracing; A time to get, and a time to lose; a time to keep, and a time to cast away; A time to rend, and a time to sew; a time to keep silent, and a time to speak; A time to love, and a time to hate; a time of war, and a time of peace."

The Season

To everything under the sun, there is a season. There are different seasons for your life. Picture your life right now. *What season are you currently going through?* Identify your season. One of the biggest challenges we go through is that we do not learn to operate in our season. There are specific times in our life that God allows us to carry out a specific assignment. There are specific times in our life when God allows us to go through a season of hurt, pain, sickness, happiness; you name it.

There was a time in Job's life when God allowed the enemy to strip Job of everything. Job's body was filled with sores; he endured a season of sickness.

All For God's Glory

Job did not sin or treat God wrongly, but God allowed him to endure this test for His glory. Maybe you are like Job going through a season of brokenness and you keep questioning God, asking Him why. Maybe you are tired, feeling depressed and confused, but let me remind you today that your season will pass. It's all for God's glory.

The Season Will Never Last Forever

There was a season in my life where I questioned God, wondering why? Why the constant delay? Why wasn't the sickness going away? Yes, I fasted, requested prayer, and did everything I knew biblically to do, but it didn't go when I wanted it to go. God didn't come through when I wanted Him to come through.

God had to take me on a journey to understand that to everything in life there is a season, and sometimes God will allow you to go through a season to bring His glory to pass in you.

Remain In The Season

One of the biggest mistakes we often make is that we try to come out of the waiting season before the time God planned to take us out. **Do not exit your season prematurely.** Sometimes we refuse to wait for God's timing because of the pain that comes from the season we're going through. So, we step out of the will of God to ease the pain of the season. I have done this so many times, and all it does is bring me right back to stage one. You cannot outrun purpose. Purpose has its time for fulfillment.

Avoid Making The Wrong Move

If you go beyond God's will by trying to exit your season before the time, you will endure double pain because you would have ended that season prematurely. Make no mistake—God will find a way to take you back to that season.

Allow God To Heal You During Your Season

Whatever your season is right now, whatever you are currently going through, try to find peace in your season. You find peace in your season by trusting the Word of God, listening to His voice, and following His command.

The key point is to listen to the voice of God. It amazes me how people often try to hear God's voice from someone or through a prophecy. Most times we tend to say, "God is not talking to me" or "I cannot hear the voice of God."

My question is, what do you understand the voice of God to mean?

God speaks through many means. He uses His people to minister to us but, most importantly, God speaks to us every single day. He takes great pleasure in speaking to us. The voice of God can be found in His Word. The Bible reminds us in **Psalm 119:105:** "Thy word *is* a lamp unto my feet, and a light unto my path." You don't need to keep searching for a prophecy when you have the prophecy right in front of you.

If you need to hear God's voice or need God to speak to you, then get in tune with the **Word of God**—that is. where His voice is most evident. His words contain power and life. No wonder it is so important to believe in the power of the spoken word.

For "In the beginning was the Word, and the Word was with God, and the Word was God" (**1 John 1:1**). Everything we need to keep us on the straight road is printed in our handbook, our tool, the **Bible**.

You will find peace by standing on the promises of God and declaring his promises over your life. Job held his integrity. Hold on to your integrity and take a stand like Job.

> **Job 27:1-6**: Moreover Job continued his parable, and said, *As* God liveth, *who* hath taken away my judgment; and the Almighty, *who* hath vexed my soul; all the while my breath *is* in me, and the spirit of God *is* in my nostrils; my lips shall not speak wickedness, nor my tongue utter deceit. God forbid that I should justify you: till I die I will not remove mine integrity from me. My righteousness I hold fast, and will not let it go: my heart shall not reproach *me* so long as I live.

Job felt every pain, every hurt, every loneliness. The Bible reminds us that when Job's friends saw him from a distance, they could not recognize him. They began to weep aloud, they tore their robes off and sprinkled dust on their heads, they sat with him seven days and seven nights without saying a word. **Job 2:11-13** tells us that Job was in a deplorable condition.

Job maintained his integrity, not because he was not hurt, but because he was a man of God's own heart.

You may be hurting now during your waiting season but maintain your integrity and be a person after God's own heart. It is just a season and it will pass.

What to do in your waiting season?

1. **You must maintain your integrity.** You must never lean to your own understanding during this period. There will be times when you do not understand why God is allowing you to go through this season. If you lean to your own understanding, you will fail. You will be constantly trying to find a way out of something you don't understand.

> **Proverbs 3:5-6:** Trust in the LORD with all thine heart; and lean not unto thine own understanding. In all thy ways acknowledge him, and he shall direct thy paths.

2. **Rest in the comfort of God** knowing that He always has a reason for allowing you to go through any season. You must understand that this is just a season and a season never last always. Seasons change, and your season will change too.

The Outcome Is Always Greater

> Beloved, think it not strange concerning the fiery trial which is to try you, as though some strange thing happened unto you: But rejoice, inasmuch as ye are partakers of Christ's sufferings; that, when his glory shall be revealed, ye may be glad also with exceeding joy (**1 Peter 4:12-13**).

Seasons will come, trials will come, suffering will come, but don't be surprised. Allow God to take you through your suffering so He may be glorified in you and your purpose will be birthed.

To Every Season, There Is A Reason

When your season is over, you will receive double for your trouble.

> And the LORD turned the captivity of Job, when he prayed for his friends: also the LORD gave Job twice as much as he had before. (**Job 42:10**).

When your season has passed, God will return to you double for your trouble. Rejoice in the Lord, because your season will birth your purpose and your purpose will lead to a life of true happiness and transformation.

Difficult seasons are never easy to endure, but God will restore you. He has done it for me and He will do it for you. My life has been a season of great trials and testing, but God kept His Word and He kept His promise. I held on to His voice and birthed ***The Pathway to Finding Purpose and Happiness.***

What do you desire to birth through this season?

Make a list and **birth your purpose through your pain.**

_____

_____

_____

_____

If you remain in your season and work with God's timing, God will allow you to birth the gift and purpose He has created you for.

May you hold on to God like Job and maintain your integrity. May you stand like the three Hebrew boys. May you wait on the Lord like David, and may He use you to birth your purpose, just as He has used me to birth mine during this season.

Let's Pray:

Heavenly Father, we come to You knowing only You alone can birth our purpose during our season. May You keep us rooted in You so the plans and the purpose You have for our life will not be aborted. Teach us how to maintain our integrity during our season so we can push through our pain and breakthrough into our purpose. In Jesus' name. Amen.

CHAPTER 15

Living On Purpose by Answering The Call

What if you were given one day to answer the call and live on purpose? What would you do?

There are many types of calls, but the call I want to speak to you about is the call of **Salvation.**

In the plan of salvation, God had you in mind. You are not a mistake, and your life is valuable.

As a child of God trying to live a Godly life, I heard about salvation but didn't understand the full effects of salvation, until one day God revealed something to me. Every aspect of our life was in the plan of salvation. When we hear about the plan of salvation, we only think about the sin God redeemed us from. But in the redemption of mankind's sin, Jesus Christ paid the ultimate cost. This price then opened the door for mankind to have complete access to the throne of God.

God now moves from saving grace to activating His plans and purpose in our life. Salvation rescues us, it redeems us, it brought us back to God, and it gave us access to carry out our divine purpose while on earth.

Let's look at the ultimate plan and purpose of salvation. In this ultimate plan of salvation, God had you in mind. (Write your name) _____ was in God's ultimate plan of salvation.

The day when He went to the cross and cried out, "It is finished" was the moment His plans and purpose for your life was completed.

My Testimony

When God gave me the mandate to write a book, many things came to my mind—thoughts like, "How will I get this book published? Where will I acquire the funds to publish a book?" The list went on and on. The thought of writing this book and not being able to publish it brought sadness to my heart. I sat for a few moments with a still heart waiting to be comforted by God.

God did it again; salvation never fails.

The spirit of God brought calmness to my soul, and He humbled me and said, "This is not about you, you are just My vessel. Before I formed you, this book was in my plan of salvation. The route of getting this book out, the finances to get it published, was already paid for on the cross."

Nothing takes God by surprise. Whatever you were created to do or accomplish is already in God's plans. One of the biggest mistakes I made was to believe that God wanted my help. **No**, God does not need our help. He has everything planned out. God desires that we live a life of obedience to His Word and fulfill our purpose on earth.

God Does Not Need Our Assistance

He said it was finished, the ultimate sacrifice was done, the pathway to get this book published was in the plan of salvation. Your purpose is a part of that plan; get to the pathway to finding your purpose so you can live a purpose-driven life and experience true happiness. The Spirit of God said, "Your job is to get my words on paper, and I will do the rest. Before I formed you in your mother's womb, I created the pathway for this book to be established."

Many times, we get worried over life's struggles simply because we do not fully understand the plan of salvation.

For every plan and purpose you were created to carry out on this earth, the path is already created for you to do it. Get connected to purpose, be obedient, and God will direct your path.

Maybe you are thinking about your future and how you will carry out the plans you have. Maybe you have even started the journey toward your future, but you are uncertain of how it will be completed.

My advice is to allow the plan of salvation to manifest in your life. Don't allow fear of the future to stop or hinder God's plans for you. Activate His promises and walk into the plans and purpose He has for your life.

He Comforted My Soul

Tears of joy begin to fall down my face. Many times we forget that it is not about us, it is about God and what He has created us to accomplish.

I may not know the plans and purpose God has for your life, but I can assure you that His plans for your life will come to pass because purpose cannot die, and the plan of salvation cannot fail.

Make a list of your plans and goals.

_____

_____

_____

_____

_____

_____

_____

Under that list, make a note that says, *"Salvation already did it."* Every time you get distracted from your purpose, look back at this last chapter and remind yourself that salvation already created the path. All you need to do is be obedient to His Word and follow His leading.

Let's Pray:

Heavenly Father, we come to You today with a humble heart, knowing that in Your plan of salvation, Your plans and purpose for my life was there. So today I ask that You calm my mind by allowing Your peace to fill my soul. Many are the plans of my heart, but, Lord, today I surrender my plans to You so that the plans and the purpose You have for my life will come to pass through the power of salvation in Jesus' name I pray. Amen.

Conclusion

Allow me to leave this final thought with you: *Don't be afraid to live the life you were created to live.* Dr. Myles Munroe made a profound statement that impacted my life tremendously. He said, "The graveyard is the richest place on earth because many died and did not accomplish their purpose."

Do you desire the graveyard to take your wealth?

One of the biggest enemies that defeat our purpose is fear. But you have the power to conqueror your fear by replacing it with your faith.

God has already qualified you for your purpose. The only way you will live a life of victory is to connect with your divine calling.

Purpose will give your life meaning, it will give you a sense of direction, and it will give you hope and a bright future.

If you desire to add meaning to your life, then purpose in your heart to live a purpose-driven life.

In whom also we have obtained an inheritance, being predestinated according to the purpose of him who worketh all things after the counsel of his own will **(Ephesians 1:11).**

May you enjoy the beauty that lies in the purpose-driven life!

Sherdeine Thomas

About the Author

Sherdeine Thomas is a Kingdom Ambassador, Minister of the Gospel, Transformational Speaker, and Christian Empowerment Life and Purpose Coach. She is also the Chief Operation Officer of Visionaries International Coaching.

As a purpose influencer, Sherdeine challenges women to take the focus off themselves and how others perceive them and empowers them to see themselves as Christ sees them. She uses her writing, speaking, coaching and mentoring to motivate women from all aspects of life to answer their calling so they can tap into their God-given potential and fulfill their divine destiny.

Her mission is to help them push through the pain and propel into their purpose. Sherdeine's greatest desire is to impact the lives of those who God connects her with and to fulfill her purpose on earth.

Download a copy of her FREE 7- Days Devotional Guide to Unleashing Your Divine Purpose E-book from her website at:

www.visionariesinternationalcoaching.com

For any other inquires re: coaching, and speaking engagements please contact Sherdeine at sherdeinethomas@gmail.com

www.ingramcontent.com/pod-product-compliance
Lightning Source LLC
LaVergne TN
LVHW051505070426
835507LV00022B/2933